you can rest here

Self-Acceptance over Self-Help

Sarah Nilson
of justfrogetaboutit

Andrews McMeel
PUBLISHING®

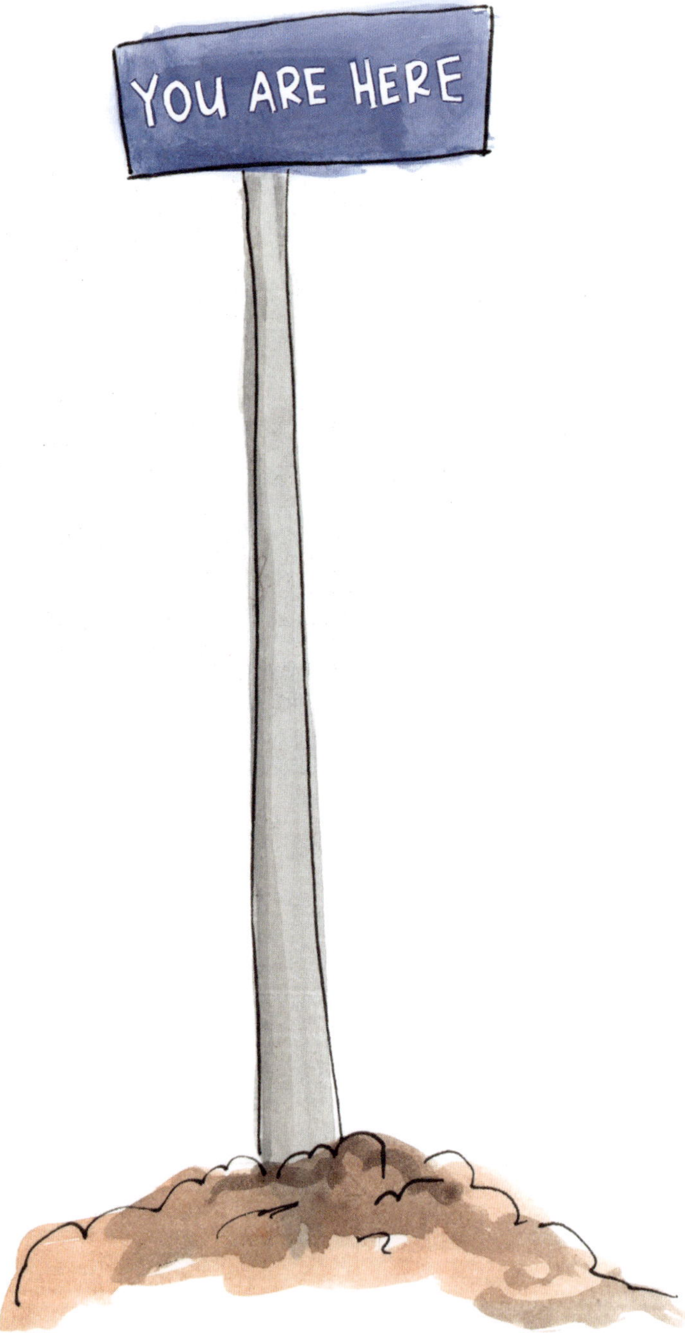
YOU ARE HERE

Yes, I am.
How does it
always know?!

Dedicated to Frankie. It's possible!

Well, hello! Happy to see YOU here!

My name is Sarah, and I'm an artist, a painter, and I guess a writer now. During the pandemic, like countless others, I lost my job in the service industry and suddenly had a lot of free time on my hands. I was restless and anxious and didn't know what to do with this vacuous space in my life that had always been filled by work. My dad, a retired painter, suggested I start painting. His exact words were, "You'll always have a job if you start working for yourself." So, without giving it too much thought and without any formal training in my back pocket, I started to paint every day. One hundred oil paintings later, I realized I was painting for my dad—looking for his approval, his love, for something to talk about with him—and not for myself.

Around this time, I watched a YouTube video by the creator Struthless called "The drawing advice that changed my life" that presented a creative challenge: Draw ONE THING every day for a year. I chose to paint a frog every day and post it on an Instagram account, @justfrogetaboutit. After weeks of drawing this same frog, something kind of magical started to happen. To keep myself interested in the challenge and make it fun, I began incorporating little jokes about what was happening in my life—qualms about dating, how I loved dogs—and the frog, named Gorf, gradually became an outlet for expressing my innermost thoughts.

And by being radically honest about the hard stuff I was butting up against in my life—fear of failure, body dysmorphia, paralyzing perfectionism—the frog evolved into an alter ego that encouraged me not only to continue painting, but to continue being honest with myself about the things that were making it impossible for me to live a full and free life. As I posted and shared the perfectly imperfect frog's journey, another kind of magical thing happened: A community of support organically formed around the messages of love, acceptance, and gentleness toward oneself at the heart of the frog-a-day project.

This book is an extension of what began online, and my hope is that you, dear reader, will embark on a journey of healing and acceptance with the frog as your flawed and fabulous inspirational guide toward happiERness. The challenge is to come as you are; to reflect with honesty—and without judgment—about your life, your fears, and behaviors that may have served you in the past but are now stumbling blocks on your path; and to strive for self-acceptance over self-help.

I make this distinction because I have always struggled with the idea of self-help and with books or programs where the inherent underlying message is that YOU ARE NOT ENOUGH. When I thought I needed the cacophony of self-help literature, I was the sickest and most miserable I had ever been. Books that shamed me into striving to do more and be more only compounded the challenges I was facing and didn't get to the root of my unhappiness. How can I help myself when I don't even like myself?

My hope is that this book guides you down a path, one frog at a time, that encourages and supports self-acceptance and self-compassion. Happiness may feel nebulous and ultimately unattainable, but acceptance and happiERness are possible and easier to digest. When we learn to accept our discomforts and our emotions and embrace the general messiness of life by practicing the art of detachment, we can learn to accept ourselves exactly as we are: whole, complete, multidimensional human beings having a totally normal human experience.

My favorite (and the most uncomfortable) aspect of this book centering around self-acceptance is that it doesn't require more from you than to just be. You don't need to wake up early, run extra miles, or buy ANOTHER self-help book. This is a mindset shift toward being gentle with yourself. Despite whatever is happening right now in front of you.

TRAIL HEAD

In a world that demands us to be fitter, better, stronger, to strive for optimization, productivity, happiness, etcetera—at least within the span of these pages, I ask you to consider an alternative. It feels as if there's this pressure to become the best possible version of ourselves. The goal isn't balance or joy, it's perfection.

At least within the
span of these pages,
I ask you to consider
the alternative.

Let's face it: We're all tired
and have enough on our plates.

If self-acceptance is the vacation we all need from the constant pressure of needing to be better, consider this a chapter-by-chapter perspective shift with the hopes of landing somewhere around radical self-acceptance by the time this book closes.

And if the feeling is fleeting, it's one you can always revisit within these pages.

INTRO

First of all, I want to start
by acknowledging,
right now in this moment—
you and I, we are safe.

Out of all the millions
of options available to you,
you have the time, space, and
safety to pick up a book, and
that's truly a blessing.

Let's drop into our bodies
before this gets heady.

What are your
shoulders doing?

Can you drop them,
away from your ears,
even if just for a moment?

Feeling the weight of
your body pressing down
on the surface beneath you.

Lengthening through your
spine, because right now
your spine is shaped
like a shrimp, bestie.

Relax your jaw,
maybe dropping
your tongue from
the roof of your mouth
for just a second.

And your
forehead and the
space between
your eyebrows.

Can you relax
that for a second?

Let that feeling run down
your body like it's a color.

Down your arms
and into your hands.

Down into your legs
and into your feet.

Nice, yeah, just like that.

Let it feel good for a minute . . .
There is no rush.

And your butt,
how's that doing?

Perfect, just as I thought.

Relax it anyway. It does not
need to be battle-ready.

Let it melt into
the seat beneath you.

Feel your feet on the ground,
wiggling your toes if you can.

Feel your fingers on the pages
and the pages on your fingers.

You can rub your thumbs inside the circles to really feel that feeling.

Feel the cool air rush by your upper lip when you take your next big inhale through your nose, then hold it at the top of your inhale.

Breathe out through your nose like you're trying to fog up a glass, totally emptying your lungs at the bottom of your exhale.

Nice.

Maybe one more
deep breath in and out
before you go.

ACCEPTANCE

The bad news is, nothing you do
will make you worthy.

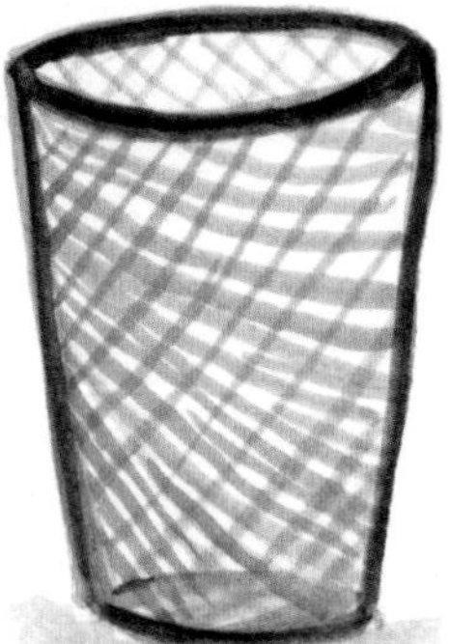

The good news is,
you don't have to do anything
to be worthy.

The paradox of self-improvement
is that at some point
it becomes self-defeating.

If I treat myself
as a project to
be worked on . . .

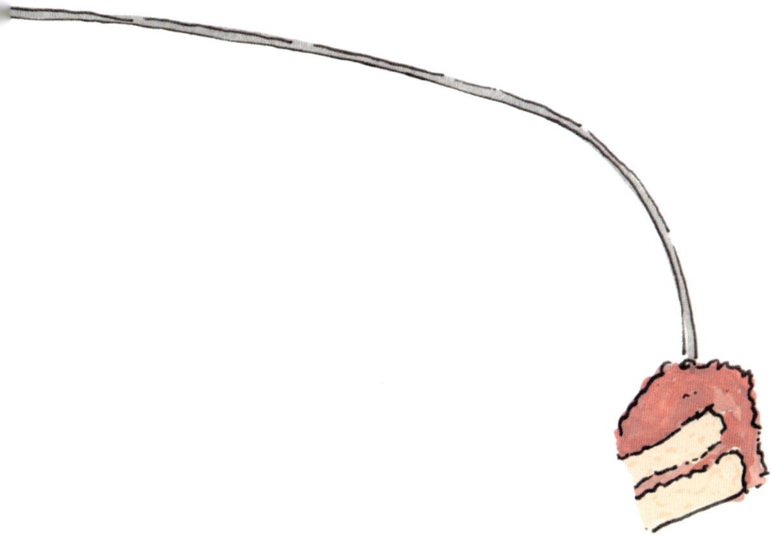

. . . there will always be work to do.

There is a pressure to constantly improve ourselves as if it's fundamentally good for us.

The truth is, no amount
of improvement
will make me perfect.

No amount of self-help
will save me from failure.

I'm not saying to completely
ditch the idea of self-help.

I'm suggesting the inverse: that when we learn to accept ourselves for who we are today . . .

. . . we can focus on self-development from a place of true fulfillment.

Imperfect action will take me further than trying to find the perfect solution.

Failure is learning
without my ego
getting involved.

And learning can be
reframed as play.

I can be a mess and
still be successful.

I can be flawed
and still be
perfectly me.

I have a lot of dreams
to chase, but today
I'm enjoying the view.

busiest
lived up to everyone's expectations
worked the most hours
rushed through it
never asked for help
rested the least
never took a break
most perfect
never said "no"

Awards that don't exist

As long as I'm trying,
I'm probably doing better
than I think I am.

Maybe the real self-improvement
isn't about how much I can do . . .

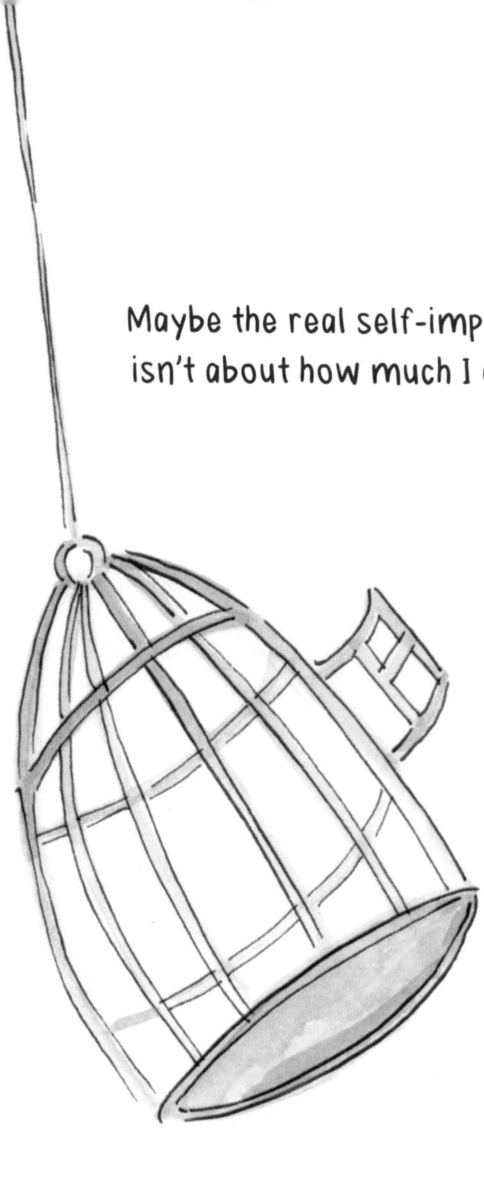

. . . but how much I can let go
of the idea that I am not
enough as I am.

SELF-TRUST

I am actively making the decision to trust my future self.

I know that I will encounter plenty of problems and missteps in my life.

I trust my future self
to handle them for me.

My future self is resilient,
resourceful, creative, and
also much more qualified
to come up with solutions
because my future self knows
what's actually going on.

As far as I know, this is
everyone's first time
being a grown-up.

I'm pretty sure we're all making it up as we go.

I am the most qualified person
to decide what feels good
to me and what feels bad to me.

Because I am a
reliable narrator of my
own existence.

GRATITUDE

This is a reminder
that gratitude is not
an inherited trait that
some are born with
and some aren't.

Feeling eternal dissatisfaction?

Maybe your gratitude muscle needs some strength training.

One way to flex your gratitude muscle is to identify things in your immediate surrounding that bring you joy.

I have a roof over my head.

I have a cozy blanket
I can wrap myself
up in every night.

I can hear birds singing
outside my window.

I have the time and
space to pick up a book.

I can take a deep breath in.

And out.

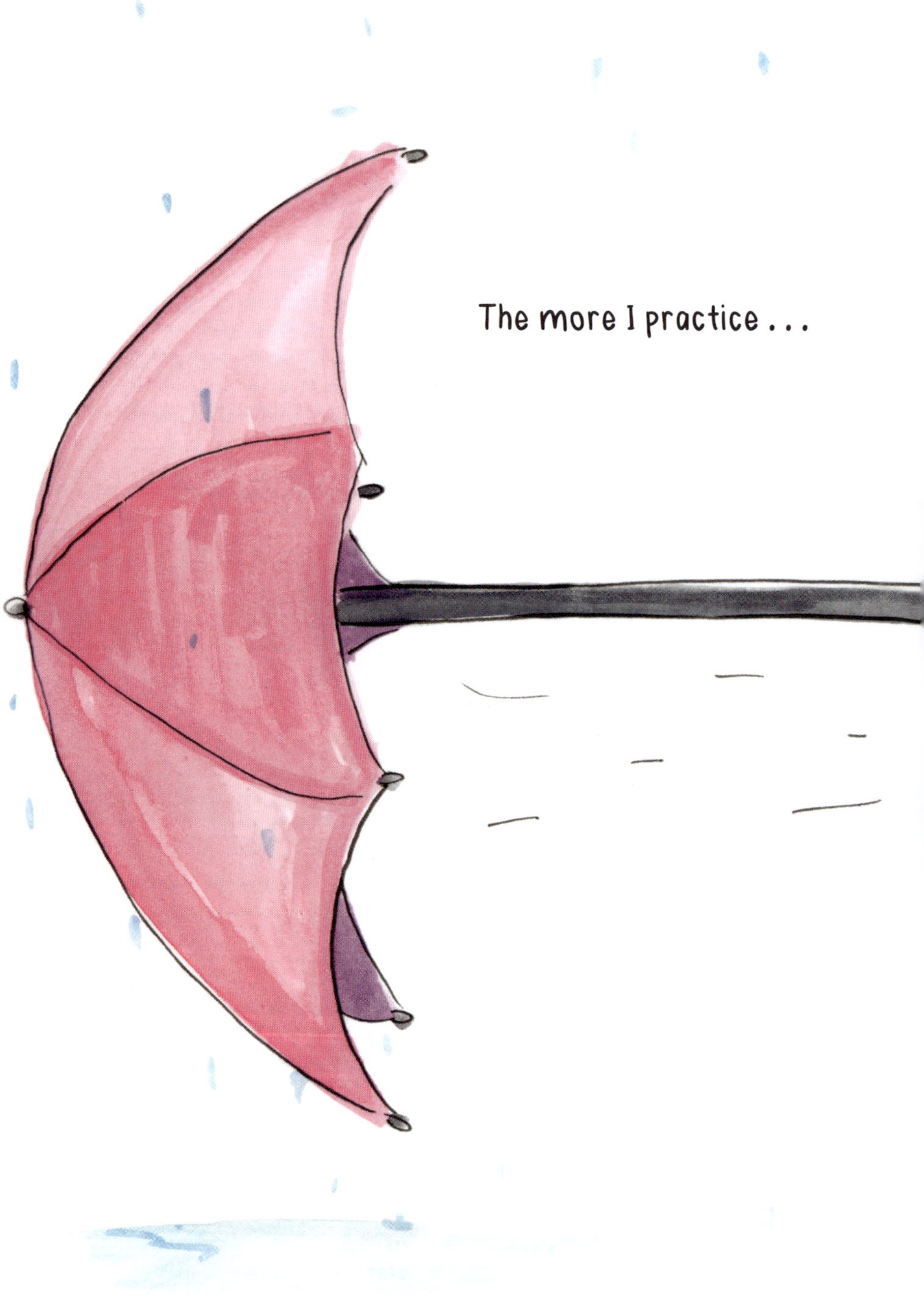

The more I practice . . .

. . . the stronger I get.

THE MUSINGS
OF IT ALL

One of the best things about being alive is that if you like a song, you can simply listen to it again.

Back-to-back, even. Like, no other song in between the song you like.

"I don't practice
Santeria, I ain't got
no crystal ball."

You can do it as much as you want
and the singer doesn't get tired.

I know a few deep breaths and a sweet treat doesn't fix everything . . .

but it does fix some stuff for a little while.

Do you know why I pulled you over?

Ommmmmmmwtfishappeningmmmmmmmm

(Repeating the same behaviors that have failed me for years) "That should do the trick!"

The Overthinker

Fart like no one's listening.

I am a human being . . .

. . . not a human doing.

The weight of being hot and funny

Just broke one of my made-up rules that only I have to follow.

Things do not get better with stress and worry.

Let it be and let it pass.

(Realizing I was wrong)
"Perhaps I was right in
a new and unusual way."

I got my spark back.

(I took a nap.)

I don't trouble trouble . . .

. . . until trouble troubles me.

The portal to every
next level is through
the parts of yourself
that you avoid.

What if I'm not silly enough?

Your challenge, should you choose
to accept it, is to spend at least
sixty seconds thinking about
all the ways you are awesome.

Permission to write
that down here if you're
into that kinda thing.

Okay bye, love you,
come back anytime.

You hate to see me go,
but I KNOW you love
to watch me leave!

The authorised representative in the EEA is Simon and Schuster
Netherlands BV, Herculesplein 96 3584 AA Utrecht, Netherlands.
(info@simonandschuster.nl)

Andrews McMeel Publishing
a division of Andrews McMeel Universal
1130 Walnut Street, Kansas City, Missouri 64106

www.andrewsmcmeel.com

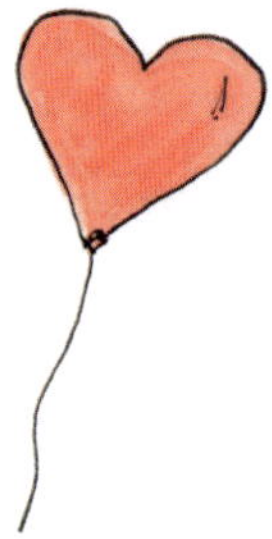

26 27 28 29 30 TEN 10 9 8 7 6 5 4 3 2 1

ISBN: 979-8-8816-0976-4

Library of Congress Control Number: 2025948995

Editor: Katie Gould
Art Director: Julie Barnes
Production Editor: Kayla Overbey
Production Manager: Julie Skalla

FSC www.fsc.org MIX Paper | Supporting responsible forestry FSC® C016973